WOMEN IN THE ARAB WORLD

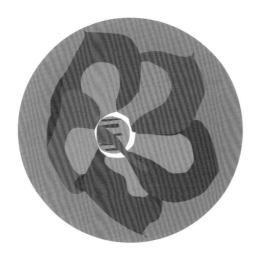

WOMEN'S ISSUES:
GLOBAL TRENDS

Women in the Arab World

Women in the World of Japan

Women in the World of Africa

Women in the World of China

Native Women in the Americas

Women in the World of India

Women in the Eastern European World

Women in the World of Southeast Asia

Women in the Hispanic World

Women in the World of Russia

Women in the Mediterranean World

Women in North America's Religious World

WOMEN'S ISSUES:
GLOBAL TRENDS

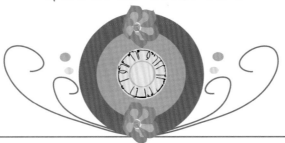

WOMEN IN THE ARAB WORLD

BY
JOAN ESHERICK

Mason Crest Publishers
Philadelphia

Mason Crest Publishers Inc.
370 Reed Road Broomall, Pennsylvania 19008
(866) MCP-BOOK (toll free)
www.masoncrest.com

First edition, 2005
13 12 11 10 09 08 07 06 05   10 9 8 7 6 5 4 3 2

Library of Congress Cataloging-in-Publication Data

Esherick, Joan.
  Women in the Arab world / by Joan Esherick.
      p. cm. — (Women's issues, global trends)
  Includes index.
          ISBN 1-59084-861-6
          ISBN 1-59084-856-X (series)
1. Women—Arab countries—Juvenile literature. I. Title. II. Series.

  HQ1784.E74 2004
  305.4'0917'4927—dc22
                        2004012709

Interior design by Michelle Bouch and MK Bassett-Harvey.
Illustrations by Michelle Bouch.
Produced by Harding House Publishing Service, Inc.
www.hardinghousepages.com
Cover design by Benjamin Stewart.
Printed in India.

CONTENTS

INTRODUCTION

by Mary Jo Dudley

The last thirty years have been a time of great progress for women around the world. In some countries, especially where women have more access to education and work opportunities, the relationships between women and men have changed radically. The boundaries between men's roles and women's roles have been crossed, and women are enjoying many experiences that were denied them in past centuries.

But there is still much to be done. On the global stage, women are increasingly the ones who suffer most from poverty. At the same time that they produce 75 to 90 percent of the world's food crops, they are also responsible for taking care of their households. According to the United Nations, in no country in the world do men come anywhere near to spending as much time on housework as women do. This means that women's job opportunities are often extremely limited, contributing to the "feminization of poverty."

In fact, two out of every three poor adults are women. According to the Decade of Women, "Women do two-thirds of the world's work, receive 10 percent of the world's income, and own one percent of the means of production." Women often have no choice but to take jobs that lack long-term secu-

rity or adequate pay; many women work in dangerous working conditions or in unprotected home-based industries. This series clearly illustrates how historic events and contemporary trends (such as war, conflicts, and migration) have also contributed to women's loss of property and diminished access to resources.

A recent report from Human Rights Watch indicates that many countries continue to deny women basic legal protections. Amnesty International points out, "Governments are not living up to their promises under the Women's Convention to protect women from discrimination and violence such as rape and female genital mutilation." Many nations—including the United States—have not ratified the United Nations' Women's Treaty.

During times of armed conflict, especially under policies of ethnic cleansing, women are particularly at risk. Murder, torture, systematic rape, forced pregnancy and forced abortions are all too common human rights violations endured by women around the world. This series presents the experience of women in Vietnam, Cambodia, the Middle East, and other war torn regions.

In the political arena, equality between men and women has still not been achieved. Around the world, women are underrepresented in their local and national governments; on average, women represent only 10 percent of all legislators worldwide. This series provides excellent examples of key female leaders who have promoted women's rights and occupied unique leadership positions, despite historical contexts that would normally have shut them out from political and social prominence.

The Fourth World Conference on Women called upon the international community to take action in the following areas of concern:

• the persistent and increasing burden of poverty on women
• inequalities and inadequacies in access to education and training
• inequalities and inadequacies in access to health care and related services

- violence against women
- the effects of armed or other kinds of conflict on women
- inequality in economic structures and policies, in all forms of productive processes, and in access to resources
- insufficient mechanisms at all levels to promote the advancement of women
- lack of protection of women's human rights
- stereotyping of women and inequality in women's participation in all community systems, especially the media
- gender inequalities in the management of natural resources and the safeguarding of the environment
- persistent discrimination against and violation of the rights of female children

The Conference's mission statement includes these sentences: "Equality between women and men is a matter of human rights and a condition for social justice and is also a necessary and fundamental prerequisite for equality, development and peace. . . equality between women and men is a condition . . . for society to meet the challenges of the twenty-first century." This series provides examples of how women have risen above adversity, despite their disadvantaged social, economic, and political positions.

Each book in WOMEN'S ISSUES: GLOBAL TRENDS takes a look at women's lives in a different key region or culture, revealing the history, contributions, triumphs, and challenges of women around the world. Women play key roles in shaping families, spirituality, and societies. By interweaving historic backdrops with the modern-day evolving role of women in the home and in society at large, this series presents the important part women play as cultural communicators. Protection of women's rights is an integral part of universal human rights, peace, and economic security. As a result, readers who gain understanding of women's lives around the world will have deeper insight into the current condition of global interactions.

THE MODERN ARAB WORLD: EXTREMES FOR WOMEN

My friends and I often discuss the difference between girls [who wear a head scarf called an abayah] and our own crowd. I wear miniskirts and hats. I date boys. I make up my hair. . . . Sometimes we see girls our age wearing the abayah. In summer, they wear these long things down to their ankles, even gloves, and we don't understand it. These are good times for women. . . . We can study what we want and choose our career. There are plenty of good jobs, especially if a girl knows a foreign language. Some girls have jobs that their boyfriends can't get. It's true that a girl [who wears an abayah] can't get a job [in some places because]. . . . Her clothes would make the people who work with her too uncomfortable. . . .

—Nilufer, a teenager, quoted in *Sandcastles: The Arabs in Search of the Modern World* by Milton Viorst

I was married at twenty-four to a cousin who was twenty-two. I didn't know him because he had been educated in the U.S. And because of that he seemed very Westernized. He even drank alcohol at the beginning. But we were no sooner married than he became a strict Islamist. I'm a good Muslim, but it is as if he went back in history. He even refused to have any furniture in the house, just carpets and cushions.

. . .He wouldn't permit a television or radio in the house. He said they

were sinful. And my friends were not allowed to visit. I was very lonely but all the time I told myself, he is my husband, my cousin, I must obey him. Whenever he wanted to have sex, we had sex. In Islam, it is not permitted for the wife to refuse her husband. And I wanted to be a good wife.

When we went out, he insisted I be completely covered, with a black veil over my face, and that I even wear gloves. I had never dressed like this before. I was not allowed outside the house without him, even to go shopping with my mother. The veil was so hot, I couldn't breathe. . . . But I did it because he wanted it. It was my duty to be compliant.

—A'isha, a woman from the United Arab Emirates, quoted in *Price of Honor* by Jan Goodwin

Our textbooks used to say the job of women was to cook and clean. Now there is enthusiasm among young women, in both the city and the countryside, to defend the country, even to join the army. Women are working at jobs they never had before. University graduates are moving all over the country to find work. This is a society that relies heavily on family and family ties. Women don't choose their husbands by themselves, and the same applies to men. The whole family participates, and we Iraqis think a good marriage is one made with the full cooperation of both families. Men and women don't separate from their families after marriage. Still it's not like the old days, in which men and women married within the tribe, or at least within the extended family. Now it is settled in Iraq that a woman can take the job she wants and, similarly, she cannot be forced to marry against her will. There is less marriage within the family than before.

—Yunis, a twenty-something Iraqi woman, quoted in *Sandcastles: The Arabs in Search of the Modern World* by Milton Viorst

> *Strong like the desert*
> *Walks like the wind*
> *Soft like the sea*
> *Her life is free*
> —poem describing a Bedouin woman

Nilufer, A'isha, Yunis, and the woman described in the preceding poem have one thing in common: they are Arab women of the twenty-first century. Though they come from different countries and families, each lives in a region heavily influenced by Arab culture. They are all women of Arab lands.

What do we mean when we use the term "Arab?" First, let's see what it does *not* mean.

"Arab" does not mean Islamic. Though Muslims (people who practice the Islamic faith) make up a majority of the people living in Arab nations, people of other faiths live among their Muslim neighbors. Thousands of Jews, Christians, Hindus, and people of other religions live in Arab nations. (See chapter 3 for more details on religion). The term "Arab" does not mean a specific religion or belief.

"Arab" also does not mean *nomad*, desert dweller, or camel herder. Do some Arabs live in the desert, sleep in tents, or sell camels for a living? Yes. But according to one estimate, more than 40 percent of people in Arab nations live in urban centers (major cities) or metropolitan areas. Many more live in villages and small towns.

So what does "Arab" mean?

Many people, including people in Arab lands, define an Arab as anyone who speaks Arabic, lives in or comes from an Arab country, and voluntarily identifies himself with Arabic culture. In this book when we use the term "Arab," we mean an Arabic-speaking person or nation located on the Arabian Peninsula or in nearby regions. To be Arab is to be part of a rich culture with centuries of history and tradition. The term "Arab" refers to this culture, including its language. Many countries, because of their shared culture, language, and heritage, have identified themselves as Arab nations.

CORRECTING COMMON MISCONCEPTIONS

- "Arab" refers to a culture, NOT a race or religion.

- Afghanistan and Iran are NOT Arab countries.

- Many faiths, not just Islam, are practiced in Arab lands.

- All Arab nations are NOT alike.

Arab nations, with combined populations of about 300 million, cover most of northern Africa and nearly all the Middle East. Most belong to an organization called the League of Arab States (also known as the Arab League). Originally founded by eight members in 1945, the Arab League today includes twenty-two governments: Algeria, Bahrain, Comoros, Djibouti, Egypt, Iraq, Jordan, Kuwait, Lebanon, Libya, Mauritania, Morocco, Oman, Palestine, Qatar, Saudi Arabia, Somalia, Sudan, Syria, Tunisia, United Arab Emirates, and Yemen, each of which shares a common language and regional heritage with the other member nations. This book's discussion of "women in Arab lands" includes women from several, but not all, of the nations represented in the Arab League.

This book also includes illustrations from the lives of women whose identity is marked more by the tribe, race, or culture (of Arab origin) from which they come than the nation in which they live. Bedouin women are one such group.

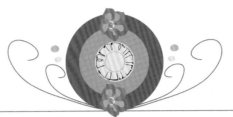

MEMBERS OF THE ARAB LEAGUE

Lebanon
Israel
Palestinian
Tunisia
Morocco
Syria
Iraq
Jordan
Kuwait
Qatar
Bahrain
Algeria
Libya
Egypt
UEA
Saudi Arabia
Oman
Mauritania
Sudan
Yemen
Somalia
Djibouti
Comoros

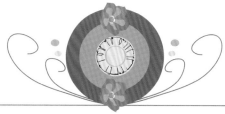

FIVE FAST FACTS ABOUT THE ARAB WORLD

FAST FACT #1: Arab lands span a geographical area of 5.25 million square miles (13.5974 square kilometers). (The United States only covers 3.6 million square miles [8.44336 square kilometers]).

FAST FACT #2: Seventy-two percent of Arab land is found in Africa.

FAST FACT #3: The great ancient civilizations of Egypt, Assyria, Babylonia, and Phoenicia originated in Arab lands.

FAST FACT #4: The world's primary monotheistic (one-God) religions were founded in Arab lands: Judaism, Christianity, and Islam.

FAST FACT #5: Of all Arab nations, Egypt has the largest population.

The Bedouins could be called the original "Arabs" and are often what non-Arabs think of when they hear the term "Arab." The Bedouins, more correctly called the *Bedu*, are a nomadic people known for their generosity, hospitality, and expertise in camel breeding and sheep and goat raising. They live in desert regions of the Middle East and northern Africa, and like other nomads, they travel from place to place in search of grazing lands and water for their herds. Bedouin women, too, are Arab women. Their rural lives, however, differ greatly from those of their urban Arab sisters. No discussion of Arab women would be complete without input from city-dwellers and rural women alike.

WHO IS THE ARAB WOMAN?

You've seen her image: dark round eyes, averted and peering from behind a dark veil; her body draped from head to toe, blending into the shadows to avoid the public eye. She is an Arab woman.

You've heard their stories: preteen girls given to men old enough to be their fathers or grandfathers, men who are already married and looking for more wives; innocent teenage virgins killed by family members because the teens were suspected of having sex before marriage; female college students strapped with bombs and AK47s destined for the next suicide mission. These, too, are Arab women.

You may have heard their names: Suzanne Mubarak, wife of the president of Egypt; Queen Rania Al-Abdallah, wife of the King of Jordan—a first lady and a queen—and both of these individuals are also women of Arab lands.

In fact, these images *all* depict women of Arab nations, yet they do not represent *the* "Arab woman." They feed the common, often mistaken, view of what it is to be a woman in the Arab world, but they don't give us the whole story. The "Arab woman" is far more complicated than brief sound bites, photographs, or five-second clips on the evening news can portray.

Despite the images we see repeated in newspapers, magazines, and on television, there is no such thing as a typical "Arab woman." To say that someone is a typical "Arab" would be like saying she is a typical "American" or typical "African" or typical "Asian" or typical "European." The lives and personalities of Arab women differ vastly from each other, just as they do in other countries and cultures. To assume that all Arab women are the same or that they experience identical joys and challenges would be to unfairly *stereotype* them. With

Bedoin women are just one type of Arab woman.

so many cultures represented in the term "Arab" (different faiths, different values, different environments, different governments, different countries), no single experience or description can capture what it means to be a woman in an Arab nation today.

To avoid misrepresenting Arab women, then, this book will include illustrations from the lives of different women in various Arab societies. What they hold in common is this: they are women; they live in the Middle East or northern Africa; they speak Arabic; and they live in a nation or culture that has identified itself as Arab. That is all. Their religions, family responsibilities, opportunities for education and vocation, and other social issues vary with the culture in which each woman lives. You may be surprised by just how different their experiences can be.

DIFFERENT NATIONS; DIFFERENT OPPORTUNITIES

Muna felt free to make her own choices. She wore pants and skirts in public. Her parents encouraged her to study. She attended college, and hoped to be a *gynecologist* someday. Though her parents suggested possible suitors, Muna had the right to refuse her parents suggestions. She could choose her future husband and her career.

Hayfa had no such choices. When she was barely eleven, her father required that she wear the *abaya* to hide her developing figure. Her family felt that education for girls beyond primary school was unnecessary since their roles confined them to the home. When Hayfa turned thirteen, her father accepted an offer of five camels for his daughter's hand in marriage. Hayfa's groom wasn't what she'd dreamed of or hoped for; at fifty-seven years old, the man Hayfa would marry was gray-haired and wrinkled and already had three wives. Islamic law allowed a man four wives if he could treat them fairly, and five camels seemed a small price to pay for a young virgin bride. Hayfa had no choice; if she refused or ran away, she would be beaten upon her return, and perhaps killed for dishonoring her family name.

Yasmin's future changed when her village opened a craft center that catered to tourists. Though the teenager never received formal schooling, her mother

TYPES OF GOVERNMENT AND LEGAL SYSTEMS IN ARAB NATIONS

COUNTRY	GOVERNMENT TYPE	LEGAL SYSTEM
Algeria	Republic	Socialist system based on French and Islamic law
Bahrain	Constitutional Hereditary Monarchy	Islamic and English common law
Comoros	Independent Republic	French and Islamic law
Djibouti	Republic	French civil law, tradition, and Islamic law
Egypt	Republic	English common law, Islamic law, and Napoleonic codes
Iraq	In transition	In transition
Jordan	Constitutional Monarchy	Islamic law and French codes
Kuwait	Nominal Constitutional Monarchy	Civil law and some Islamic law
Lebanon	Republic	Mixture of Ottoman law, canon law, Napoleonic law and civil law
Libya	Military Dictatorship	Italian civil law and Islamic law
Mauritania	Republic	Combination of Islamic law and French civil law
Morocco	Constitutional Monarchy	Islamic law and French and Spanish civil law
Oman	Monarchy	English common law and Islamic law
Qatar	Traditional Monarchy	Discretionary law controlled by Amir (king)
Saudi Arabia	Monarchy	Islamic law
Somalia	No permanent national government	Transitional, parliamentary national government; no national system of law
Sudan	Authoritarian military regime	Islamic law on all people (regardless of religion) in northern states, otherwise combination of Islamic law and English common law
Syria	Republic under a military regime	Islamic law and civil law system
Tunisia	Republic	Based on French civil law and Islamic law
United Arab Emirates	Federation of member states	Federal court system
Yemen	Republic	Based on Islamic, Turkish, English, and tribal law

Some Arab women are heavily robed whenever they are in public.

trained her in the fine art of bead craft. Yasmin learned to make intricate earrings, necklaces, and bracelets, and her skill gave her a source of independent income. As a Bedouin, Yasmin also had the freedom to choose a husband, and to leave him if he mistreated her.

$\mathcal{M}$una, Hayfa, and Yasmin all live in Arab lands.

Arab nations today are not the same, nor do they afford the same opportunities for women. In some Arab nations, women hold public office, vote in elections, attend college and graduate schools, pursue careers of their choosing, remain single if they want, and dress how they wish. In other Arab nations, women cannot drive cars, are forced to marry, cannot leave their homes without their spouses or male family members, cannot hold jobs outside the home, and cannot attend school or vote in elections. Opportunities for Arab women vary with the government and legal system used in each country.

In some Arab nations, the law forbids a husband to beat or otherwise physically harm his wife. In others, a husband can legally torture, maim, or kill his wife or daughter if he suspects her of *promiscuity*.

In some Arab nations, women live with *civil rights* nearly equal to those of men. In others, women have little or no rights at all.

In some Arab nations, women become poets, novelists, teachers, doctors, physicians, chemists, engineers, judges, lawyers, journalists, and representatives in government. In others, women may not even learn to read.

The experiences of women in today's Arab nations are as different as the nations and cultures themselves. Women like Nilufer, whose comments opened this chapter, can look forward to a future filled with opportunities. Women like A'isha, whose husband's wishes severely restricted her participation in public life, have fewer choices. Nomadic Arab women like Yasmin have even fewer options and face even greater risks.

Despite their varying challenges, women in Arab nations have distinguished themselves, as have women of other nations, not only in modern times but in ages past. In the next chapter we'll learn about history's most outstanding Arab women and how their lives influenced their cultures and impacted countless Arab women over the centuries.

ARAB WOMEN IN AGES PAST

One woman owned property; another did not.

One woman could divorce her husband; another could not.

One woman taught religious *doctrine* to men; another's faith forbade her from doing so.

The experiences and opportunities of Arab women in the past varied depending on culture, religious faith, and government laws just as they do today. Whether in Ancient times or the Middle Ages, women's fates often rested in the hands of their societies, and those societies' leaders included mostly men. Laws and views of women have changed throughout the history of the Arab world.

ANCIENT ASSYRIA

Ancient civilizations, in some instances, gave women greater rights and freedoms than some Arab governments do today. Laws in the kingdom of Assyria, for example, which three thousand years ago covered much of southeastern

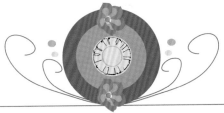

SELECT ASSYRIAN LAWS REGARDING WOMEN

The ancient Assyrians recorded their laws in a book called the **Code of the Assura**. Here are some excerpts from the Code regarding women:

"I.2: If a woman bring her hand against a man, they shall prosecute her; 30 manas of lead shall she pay, 20 blows shall they inflict on her."

"I.9: If a man bring his hand against the wife of [another] man, treating her like a child, and they prove it against him, and convict him, one of the man's fingers they shall cut off. If he kiss [another man's wife], his lower lip with the blade of an axe they shall draw down and they shall cut off."

"I.12: If the wife of a man be walking on the highway, and a man . . .seize her and by force rape her . . . the elders shall . . . put him to death. There is no punishment for the woman."

Asia and the northern Arabian peninsula (portions of today's Iraq, Syria, and Jordan), gave women greater protection against sexual assault than laws in present-day Jordan. According to the *Code of the Assura* (the laws of the Assyrian empire), if a man forced a married woman (not his wife) to have sex against her will, the rapist would be put to death and the woman would receive no punishment. Present-day Jordanian law views rape as the woman's fault, often leaving her "punishment" up to her family. Common punishments for being a Jordanian rape victim include disfigurement (cutting off her nose and ears), beatings, and death. Since women today have no legal way to charge a man with rape in Jordan, the rapist often goes unpunished.

Marriage laws in ancient Assyria were not as liberated as Assyrian sexual assault laws. The Code gave men the right to beat their wives: "Unless it is forbidden in the tablets, a man may strike his wife, pull her hair, her ear he may bruise or pierce. He commits no misdeed thereby" (Code of Assura, I.58). But if a woman in quarrel with a man injured one of the man's testicles, one of her fingers would be cut off; if she injured both testicles, she'd lose both of her eyes (Code of Assura, I:8). If a woman's husband committed a crime, she bore the same responsibility as her husband for his acts, even if she did no wrong. The courts gave her the same punishment her husband received, including death: ". . . and crimes of the husband she shall bear as if she too committed them" (Code of Assura, I.32). Women in ancient Assyria could literally die for their husband's misdeeds.

Women in Assyria also had to cover their heads and faces if they went outdoors. Only prostitutes could go without veils, and laws commanded them to do so. If a prostitute or maidservant put on a veil, officials could strip them of their garments, inflict fifty blows, and pour bitumen (crude petroleum or tar) over their heads.

Women in Egypt fared better than their Assyrian sisters.

Ancient Egypt left behind great archeological reminders of its culture.

WOMEN IN THE ARAB WORLD

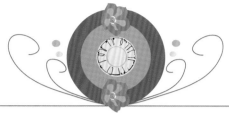

RESPECTED ARAB WOMEN FROM THE ANCIENT PAST

Queen Kemut (Cleopatra) (first century B.C.): the most powerful Egyptian queen whose leadership made Egypt the strongest nation of its time. She spoke many languages, and chose to commit suicide instead of losing her kingdom to Roman invaders.

Aisha (seventh century A.D.): the youngest (and only virgin) of the Prophet Muhammad's wives (his other wives were war widows), known for her intelligence, charm, and devotion to the Prophet. Muslims revere her as the mother of all believers.

Zaynab Bint 'Ali (seventh century A.D.): the Prophet Muhammad's grand-daughter who, after being captured by enemies, confronted her captors about their unjust ways.

Rabi'ah Al-Adawiyyah (eighth century A.D.): Islamic woman known for her holiness, who taught Muslims about divine love and intimacy with God.

Narisah (ninth century A.D.): famous figure from Islamic history who spent much of her life fasting, praying, and reciting the Qur'an (Koran). She fled to Egypt to avoid persecution and was buried in Cairo. Her tomb is a shrine today.

Arab script.

WOMEN IN THE ARAB WORLD

ANCIENT EGYPT

Women in ancient Egypt (fourth century B.C.) owned and managed private property. They bought and sold land, slaves, servants, livestock, and market goods. They managed family and business money. Women enjoyed the same legal and economic rights as the men of their same social class. When an Egyptian girl married, she kept her own assets and independent legal status; anything she brought with her to the marriage remained hers and could not be taken from her.

By contrast, in Saudi Arabia today, even though religious law and social custom allow women to own property, other laws make it difficult for women to conduct business. According to the U.S. State Department's 2003 Country Report on Human Right's Practices in Saudi Arabia, women may not use public facilities when men are present, must board city buses by separate rear entrances, and must sit in specially designated sections in the back of the bus. Law and custom forbid women to travel in the country or out of the country alone. Ancient Egyptian women ventured further into the business world than today's Saudi women.

PRE-ISLAMIC TIMES

Over the course of the Middle East's development, women's status worsened. Compared with their ancestors, Middle Eastern women of later centuries held less value. A woman had little or no rights apart from those connected to her spouse or father. Custom still required that women cover their heads or faces (or both) in public, and that she honor male leadership with uncompromising obedience. All women required a male overseer, whether her husband, father, brother, or son. Even religious traditions encouraged a lesser view of women by consigning her to specific roles.

In Middle East Jewish traditions, for example (though not technically considered Arab, but occurring in some Arab lands), Jewish women could not enter the same sections of the Temple (the Jewish place of worship) as men. A common Jewish prayer among Orthodox Jewish men of ancient times expressed gratitude that God "has not made me a woman." This expression occurred as part of a broader expression of thanks for the privilege of obeying God's law, as written in the Torah. Since the Torah was taught expressly to men, and gave far more instructions to men, the prayer expressed gratitude for the man's greater religious responsibility. Women in Jewish tradition, though highly valued as wives and mothers, faced too many societal and cultural restrictions to list here. Ultimately, Jewish patriarchal society (led by men) restricted women's roles.

The teachings of Jesus Christ in the first century A.D. violated many of his culture's traditions. Though a Jew himself, he treated women very differently from what Jewish tradition allowed. The New Testament Bible (the Christian Holy Scriptures) records that Jesus welcomed women to his teachings. It describes instances where women touched him without his objection. He forgave women when Jewish law required their punishment. After his death, the New Testament states that women were the first to witness the empty tomb after Jesus' resurrection and to carry that news to others. It also cites women in the early Christian church holding positions of much higher responsibility than existing culture or custom allowed: some carried letters from teachers to various churches and presented these letters to groups of men and women. Still others instructed men in the faith (previously unheard of in a one-god religion). Jesus Christ modeled a high view of women, and that higher view resulted in some (though not many) privileges being granted to women of that time, especially in the Christian church. As a result, many women in Arab lands embraced the Christian faith. Some even became *martyrs*.

In Tunisia (an Arab nation), a Christian Tunisian woman named Vibia Perpetua refused to perform a sacrifice honoring the Roman emperor and became one of the earliest Christian martyrs. Roman leaders condemned her to death in Carthage in 203 B.C., but a record of her experiences while in prison wasn't discovered until the seventeenth century. Tunisian Christians today revere this Arab woman for her faith.

SEVENTH-CENTURY ARABIAN PENINSULA

Most Arabs view the Prophet Muhammad as a great liberator of women. During the late 500s A.D., societies in Asia Minor, Northern Africa, and the Arabian Peninsula treated women as little more than property. Fathers grieved if a daughter was born instead of a son, and many cultures practiced infanticide (the killing of newborn babies) when a mother gave birth to a girl. Invading armies captured women and girls to make them slaves. Parents offered daughters as sacrifices to pagan gods. Fathers traded daughters away in business transactions. Families arranged marriages, forcing daughters as young as eight or nine years of age to marry men chosen by their fathers. Their cultures and laws denied women of the seventh century any choice in these matters. In many regions, disobeying, running away, or refusing to cooperate meant death.

Muhammad and the beginning of Islam changed the status of women in that region by issuing new laws based on the revelation (recorded in the Qur'an) Muhammad claimed to have received from God. In contrast to many existing customs of that time, the Qur'an gave women the right to refuse a marriage proposal, the right to receive an inheritance, the right to own property, and the right to ask for a divorce. It instructed fathers to celebrate their daughters' births, to view them as gifts from God, to provide for them as they would their sons, and to educate them (unheard of in that time). But Islamic law based on the Qur'an, which is largely the same today as it was when it was issued by Muhammad fourteen hundred years ago, doesn't treat women as fairly or as equitably as it seems.

Yes, a woman could ask for a divorce, but she had to prove to a special court that her husband treated her inappropriately. Her husband could claim that any abuse his wife suffered was just physical discipline he used according to the Qur'an's instructions (the Qur'an allows men to punish wives for disobedience). The courts usually believed the husband's claim and rarely granted the woman's request. A man, on the other hand, could summarily divorce his wife just by saying so, without reason.

Yes, a woman could receive an inheritance, but it could only be half of what her male relatives received.

Yes, a woman could technically refuse a marriage proposal, but cultural and social pressures often forced her to comply with her parents' wishes.

Yes, a woman could own property, but the only property truly belonging to her were the gifts she received from her husband at marriage and her *dowry* (though even this was sometimes forfeited in a divorce).

Islam did, however, encourage a higher view of women than many primitive cultures of the early seventh century. But women still had a long way to go.

THE MODERN AGE

Fast forward through twelve hundred years. Why is history so silent during these years? Women in the Arab world had lower legal status than men for most of the first and second millennia. Women could not vote or hold office, nor could women testify in court. On the rare occasions when a woman's testimony was needed, her testimony counted only half as much as a man's. Because women officially held lower societal status, they worked behind the scenes, primarily supporting or influencing male leaders. Though records from the Middle Ages recount instances where women led armies in battles or negotiated their own marriage contracts, women in Arab history remained largely overlooked in historical documentation. Certain exceptions exist, but few his-

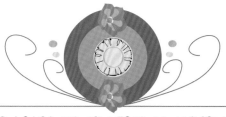

Hoda Sha'rawi (early twentieth century): pioneer of Egyptian women's rights, political activist, and founder of the Arab Women's Association.

Golda Meir (mid/late twentieth century): once lived in Palestine and worked to establish a Jewish state; prime minister of Israel from 1969 to 1974.

Um Khulthoum (twentieth century): well-known Egyptian singer who began her career as a child by singing verses from the Qur'an.

torians recorded the lives, teaching, and influence of Arab women, especially during the second millennium. That changed in the 1800s.

Hoda Sha'rawi, an Egyptian girl born in 1879 to a politically powerful family, demonstrated remarkable intelligence and discipline by committing the entire Qur'an to memory when she was only eight years old. When her father died, her education, training, and upbringing fell into her mother's hands. Private teachers tutored her in science, painting, music, arts, and several languages. The

Hoda Sha'rawi

girl learned quickly and easily, and her intellect captured the attention of her famous, politically active cousin who later married her.

The status and privilege that came with being married to a rich, powerful man gave Hoda Sha'rawi the opportunity to dedicate her life to social service and political change. She organized demonstrations; she founded and published two women's magazines; she advocated for women's equal rights; she headed the first women's society in Egypt; and she held office in international women's associations. She led the first women's demonstration in Egypt in 1919 and encouraged women to participate in public activities as much as the law would allow. Her participation in international conferences boosted the status of Egyptian women in ways that would previously not even have been considered. She strived for (and accomplished) the raising of the legal marrying age for Egyptian girls to age sixteen, *advocated* education for girls, and was instrumental in the opening of the first Egyptian secondary school for girls in 1924. She dedicated her life to improving the status, welfare, and opportunities for Egyptian women and women of other Arab lands.

Though Arab women throughout history experienced varying persecution as well as varying freedom, the most telling status of women in Arab lands today are their roles in contemporary religious cultures. The next chapter takes a look at this issue.

RELIGION AND ARAB WOMEN

Nine-year-old Fatima wakes to the sound of the *adhan*, the call to morning prayer, as it is broadcast from the tall slender tower of her local *mosque*. Though the sun has not yet risen, the *muezzin*'s voice pulses through the air:

"Allahu akbar, Allahu akbar!" *God is most great, God is most great! I testify that there is no god but God. I testify that there is no god but God. I testify that Muhammad is the Messenger of God. I testify that Muhammad is the Messenger of God. Hasten to prayer. Hasten to prayer. Hasten to prosperity. Hasten to prosperity. Prayer is better than sleep. Prayer is better than sleep. God is most great, God is most great. There is no god but God.*

Loudspeakers broadcast the adhan, minus its phrases about sleep, again at noon, in late afternoon, at sunset, and after dark. The call punctuates Fatima's day as it does that of most Arabs. In nations whose populations are primarily Islamic, businesses and shops close with this call to prayer to allow Muslims to stop their daily activities and pray.

Prayer is one of several practices common to most faiths of Arab lands, though the how, when, and means of prayer differ from faith to faith. The

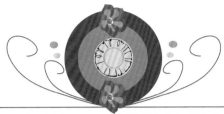

PERCENTAGE OF PEOPLE PRACTICING SPECIFIC FAITHS IN ARAB LANDS

\Algeria: 99% Islam (Sunni)

Bahrain: 100% Islam (70% Shi'ite, 30% Sunni)

Comoros: 98% Islam (Sunni); 2% Roman Catholicism

Djibouti: 94% Islam; 6% Christianity

Egypt: 94% Islam; 6% Christianity

Iraq: 97% Islam (60–65% Shi'ite, 32-37% Sunni); 3% Christianity or other

Jordan: 92% Islam; 6% Christianity; 2% other

Kuwait: 85% Islam (30% Shi'ite, 70% Sunni); 15% Christianity, Hinduism, and other

Lebanon: 70% Islam; 30% Christianity (also traces of Judaism)

Libya: 100% Islam

Mauritania: 100% Islam

Morocco: 98.7% Islam; 1.1% Christianity; 0.2% Judaism

Oman: 95% Islam

Palestine (West Bank): 75% Islam; 17% Judaism; 8% Christianity and other

Palestine (Gaza Strip): 98.7% Islam; 0.7% Christianity; 0.6% Judaism

Qatar: 95% Islam

Saudi Arabia: 100% Islam

Somalia: 100% Islam (Sunni)

Sudan: 70% Islam (Sunni); 20% various indigenous faiths, 5% Christianity

Syria: 90% Islam; 10% Christianity

Tunisia: 98% Islam (Sunni), 1% Christianity; less than 1% Judaism

United Arab Emirates: 96% Islam (80% Sunni, 16% Shi'ite); 4% others

Yemen: 100% Islam (Sunni and Shi'ite)

The call to prayer is broadcast from these minarets to faithful Muslims in the surrounding city.

three primary religious faiths practiced in Arab countries are Islam, Judaism, and Christianity. In this region of the world, Judaism (the religion of the Jewish people) and Christianity (the religion of those who believe in Jesus Christ) are minority religions. By far, the most common religion in Arab nations is Islam. Many Arab nations, especially those where Islam is the official national religion, forbid public expressions of other faiths.

The U.S. Department of State's Consular Information Sheet on Saudi Arabia states that "public non-Muslim religious services are illegal, and public display of non-Islamic religious articles such as crosses and Bibles is not permitted. Travel to Makkah (Mecca) and Medina, the cities where the two holiest mosques of Islam are located, is forbidden to non-Muslims." That includes

WHERE DO MOST MUSLIMS LIVE?

Believe it or not, of countries in the world with the largest Muslim populations, only one (Egypt) is an Arab nation. The countries with the most Muslims include: Indonesia, Pakistan, Bangladesh, India, Turkey, Iran, Egypt (an Arab nation), Nigeria, and China.

What lesson do we find in this statistic? Even though most Arabs may be Muslim, most Muslims are not Arabs.

WOMEN IN THE ARAB WORLD

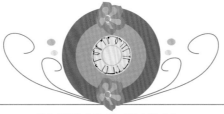

- Over one billion people in the world practice Islam.

- Only 18 percent of the world's Muslims live in Arab lands.

- Thirty percent of the world's Muslims live in South Asia.

- Twenty percent of the world's Muslims live in Sub-Saharan Africa.

- Nearly six million Muslims live in America.

- Islam is the fastest growing religion in the United States.

- The largest Muslim community is in Indonesia.

tourists. The Saudi government generally allows non-Muslims (Christians and Jews) to practice their faith in private, just not in public places. Christians and Jews in Morocco, on the other hand, can practice their faith publicly, but they cannot try to *convert* someone. In Lebanon, freedom of religious conversation and choice is guaranteed. Other Arab nations are not as tolerant.

In Jordan and Kuwait, legal code makes it illegal to discuss Christianity or for a Muslim to convert to Christianity. Even in Morocco, which tolerates other faiths, laws forbid Muslims from converting to the Christian faith. The United Arab Emirates, though it allows people to worship as they choose, forbids proselytizing of any kind (trying to convince someone else to believe your faith).

Because Islam is the most common religion in most Arab nations, it is practiced by most Arab women.

AN OVERVIEW OF ISLAM

Islam is one of the three major monotheistic religions of the world. Like Judaism (the Jewish faith) and Christianity (the Christian faith), Islam honors one God (*mono* = "one"; *theistic* = "having to do with god"). Muslim teaching states that Judaism, Christianity, and Islam worship the same God and come from the same historic lineage: that of the biblical figure Abraham. According to Judaism, however, Abraham is the *patriarch* of the Jewish nation, chosen by God to father a people who would be set apart for God's special purposes. The Christian faith affirms God's original choosing of Abraham and Israel, but views Jesus Christ (a direct descendant of Abraham) as the expected Jewish Messiah and Savior of the world. (Jews reject Jesus as their Messiah.) These are the important differences between these three monotheistic religions.

Islam reveres Abraham and Jesus Christ as honored messengers from God, but it views Muhammad, a prophet born in the late sixth century, as the final Prophet and supreme Messenger. According to Islam, God's words to Muhammad are the last and most *authoritative* words from God to human beings. Muslims believe Muhammad is a direct descendent of Abraham, too, but that he comes from a different branch of Abraham's family tree than the line that led to Moses, the Jewish King David, and Jesus Christ.

The term Muslim, which in Arabic means "a person who has surrendered to God," describes someone who practices the religion called *Islam.* The word "islam" in Arabic means "submission to God." Though "islam" originally meant an attitude that recognized God as in charge of all things and described the in-

A Brief Comparison of Islam, Judaism, and Christianity

	ISLAM	JUDAISM	CHRISTIANITY
Date started (approximate)	A.D. ~620	B.C. ~2250	A.D. ~30
Founder	Muhammad	Abraham	Jesus Christ
Where begun	what is today Saudi Arabia	Mesopotamia	Israel
Holy Scriptures	the Qur'an (God's sayings to Muhammad), and the Hadith (Muhammad's sayings)	the Torah, other writings, and the Talmud (oral tradition)	the Bible (the Old and New Testaments)
Primary day of worship	Friday	Saturday	Sunday
Main place of worship	Mosque	Temple	Church
Life after death?	Yes. Judgment before God, followed by either paradise or hell.	Yes, but not immediate. Will have eternal life when the Messiah comes.	Yes. Judgment before God, followed by either heaven or hell.
Means to obtain heaven/paradise	Not guaranteed, but pleasing Allah by doing good works to make up for bad deeds gives one hope for heaven.	Assumes all Israel will be in heaven; good deeds ensure greater shares of heaven (evil deeds can cause lost shares of heaven).	Eternal life is not earned; believes that Jesus Christ died in order to offer eternal life to all people.

The star and the crescent is a symbol for Islam. It is also featured on the flags of several Muslim nations.

ternal peace that came with that recognition, the term today (when capitalized, as in "Islam") identifies a specific set of religious beliefs attributed to the record of God's words spoken by the archangel Gabriel to Muhammad.

A book called the Qur'an, the holy book of the Islamic faith, records these words. The Qur'an (God's words to Muhammad) and another book called the Hadith (a collection of Muhammad's sayings, teaching, and recorded actions) dictate the rules by which Muslims (and most Arabs) live, including the rules for women.

THE QUR'AN, THE HADITH, AND WOMEN

Most Muslims will tell you that Muhammad was the first true *feminist*—a surprising assertion considering that the Prophet had at least ten wives, the youngest of which was six years old when he married her and only nine years old when he first had sexual intercourse with her. Despite these facts, Muhammad did much to elevate the status of women in his day. Through his writings and the Qur'an, Muhammad taught that:

1. God made men and women equal in value (but different in roles).
2. Women and men alike could practice the Islamic faith.
3. Parents should celebrate the birth of daughters (instead of mourning them or killing them as was customary at that time) and encourage their education.
4. Women could reject a marriage proposal.
5. A woman could inherit and own property independently of her father, husband, brother, son, or other family member.

The select teachings from the Qur'an listed above, if looked at alone, might make Islam seem to liberate women. These teachings, however, don't provide the complete picture. We will discuss the specifics of women in Arab cultures

(including marriage, divorce, parenting, etc.) in later chapters in this book, but for now, let's look at other teachings of Islam (taken directly from the Qur'an) that heavily influenced the Arab world:

- Muhammad taught that women had rights similar to men, but that men were ultimately stronger and had more authority: *And they (women) have rights similar to those (of men) over them, and men a degree above them (women)* (Qur'an 2:228).
- Muhammad taught that men could marry up to four wives (but women could only have one husband): *And if you fear that you cannot act equitably towards orphans, then marry such women as seem good to you, two and three and four; but if you fear that you will not do justice (between them), then (marry) only one or what your right hands possess; this is more proper, that you may not deviate from the right course* (Qur'an 4:2-3).
- Muhammad taught that men could admonish their wives, refuse to share a bed with them, and beat them (lightly, so as not to injure them). *Men are the maintainers of women because Allah has made some of them to excel others and because they spend out of their property; the good women are therefore obedient, guarding the unseen as Allah has guarded; and (as to) those on whose part you fear desertion, admonish them, and leave them alone in the sleeping-places and beat them; then if they obey you, do not seek a way against them; surely Allah is High, Great* (Qur'an 4:34).

After reading the above passages would you say that Islam liberates or oppresses women? The answer isn't clear.

People all over the world debate what Islam teaches about women. Much controversy exists about what is truly found in Islamic teachings and what is

ancient tradition or culture. One thing about which all Muslims agree is the right of Muslim women to practice the five pillars of the Islamic faith.

ISLAM'S FIVE PILLARS

To follow Islam properly, good Muslims must carry out five basic duties: profess the faith; practice ritual prayer; give to the poor, fast (*abstain* from food, drink, smoking, and sex) during daylight hours for the month of Ramadan;

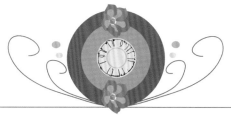

THE FIVE PILLARS OF ISLAM

The "Five Pillars of Islam" describe the basic duties every Muslim must practice to be a good follower of Islam:

1. Shahada: Believing and professing the statement of faith: "There is no god but God, and Muhammad is the Messenger of God."

2. Salat: Saying regular prayers at specified times.

3. Zakat: Giving to the poor.

4. Sawm: Practicing daylight fasts during Ramadan, the ninth month of the lunar calendar.

5. Hajj: If physically and financially able, traveling to Mecca during the Great Hajj once in a lifetime.

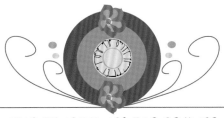

THE FIVE TIMES FOR PRAYER
(SALAT: THE SECOND PILLAR)

Dawn (fajr): between the break of dawn and sunrise

Midday (zuhr): anytime from when the sun passes its highest

point in the sky to when a shadow becomes the same length as

its object.

Late afternoon (asr): anytime from when a shadow becomes

the same length as its object to just before the sun begins to set

Sunset (maghrib): anytime from after sunset to until it is dark

Nighttime (isha): anytime from darkness to the start of morning

twilight.

and, if able, travel to the holy city of Mecca once in their lives. Islam requires women, like men, to do all five.

The profession of faith is simply a statement of belief. Muslims around the world recite the following phrase to state what they believe (translated from Arabic into English): *"There is no god but God, and Muhammad is the Messenger of God."* The Arabic word for "God" is *Allah.* Professing this statement, volun-

tarily and with full belief, makes a person a Muslim. But belief alone isn't enough. The next pillar is prayer.

Ritual prayer occurs five times per day, and all Muslims are expected to stop what they are doing, kneel in the direction of the city of Mecca, and pray. Many Muslims go to their local mosques (places of worship) for ritual prayer (women pray in separate sections of the mosque away from the men), but these prayers can technically be done anywhere. A woman, like a man, must make sure she is "clean" before she prays. She must wash according to the laws of her faith, remove her shoes, and cover her entire body (except her face and hands).

Other aspects of Islamic prayer require special rules for women. Because blood is considered unclean in Islam, when a Muslim woman menstruates or bleeds from the birth of a child, she is not allowed to pray, fast, or touch (and in some places recite) the Qur'an. At no time does Islam allow her to pray in

WATCH YOUR TERMS!

Arab, Muslim, and Islam are not interchangeable terms:

"Arab" describes a culture.

"Islam" describes a religion.

"Muslim" describes a person who practices Islam.

Muslims stop what they are doing five times a day in order to kneel in prayer toward the city of Mecca.

the same room with men. Women who attend mosques find themselves relegated to distant spaces behind a curtain, in a balcony, or in a separate room away from the men and beyond the voice of the spiritual leader (imam). In Islam, women cannot teach men, so Muslim women who have trained in the ways of Islam teach only girls and other women.

The greater corporate worship (when Muslims go to the mosque to pray together as a group) occurs during noon prayers on Fridays. Islam requires only men to go to the mosque at this time; Islam encourages women to pray at home.

In addition to prayer, Islam requires Muslim women and men to fast during daylight hours during Ramadan, the ninth month of the lunar calendar. In most Arab nations, vast majorities of the population participate in this annual time of refraining from food, drink, smoking, and sex. Businesses stay open fewer hours, some close completely, and the entire pace of life slows down. The only exception for fasting is if a woman is pregnant or nursing, or if a person (man or woman) is unable to fast for health reasons.

Like Muslim men, the women of Islam try to make one trip to the holy city of Mecca sometime in their lives. Islamic law, surprisingly, states that women should *not* be veiled during this pilgrimage; instead, their faces are supposed to remain uncovered. Once in Mecca and while at various shrines, men and women mix together equally in the crowd. Women do not have to be separated from men during this time in their spiritual journey. The pilgrimage to Mecca seems to be the one place in Islam where men and women stand on equal ground.

"IN ARAB SOCIETY, . . . A YOUNG WOMAN, AND BY ASSOCIATION, HER FAMILY, IS CONSIDERED HONORABLE IF SHE HAS MAINTAINED HER CHASTITY UNTIL MARRIAGE."—WILLIAM G. BAKER

ARAB WOMEN AND THE PUBLIC WORLD

Maysam lives in Saudi Arabia. Her family lives comfortably in an urban apartment. She has a graduate degree, and works outside the home. She cannot, however, drive herself to work, leave the house alone, travel outside the country without official permission from her husband, or ride a bike in her neighborhood. Because of laws forbidding these actions, a hired driver chauffeurs Maysam to work each day; she never ventures out of the house alone; when she must travel for business, her husband signs a letter allowing her to do so; and bike riding? She just doesn't do it.

Rushd lives in Jordan. Married at sixteen to a distant cousin she barely knew, she cannot read or write, but she brought great honor to her family and husband by bearing three sons in less than four years. Rushd, however, almost never leaves her home. Fearing her husband's beatings if he so much as suspects that she looks at another man, Rushd prefers to stay secluded behind the walls of her family compound, completely isolated from other men. She lives in fear of her husband's suspicious nature, knowing that any accusation, even if untrue, could lead to her death.

Both women live in Arab countries, yet their lives are very different. One seems free, the other confined, yet each lives under laws that govern what she can and cannot do.

Most people in Arab nations, though not all, practice Islam, and most Arab governments include at least some *tenets* of the Islamic faith in their laws. Despite the widespread popularity of Islam in Arab lands, most Arab governments use only parts of Islamic law to govern. They combine these laws with English, tribal, and *colonial* laws to create a guide for their legal systems. Only a few Arab nations, like Saudi Arabia and Sudan, use systems based almost exclusively on Islam. Islamic nations (countries who base their laws on Islam) do not separate religion from politics, business, education, family life, or commerce. Rather, religion dictates every sphere of life, including a woman's appearance and behavior in public places.

Islamic law requires women to act, dress, and live according to strict codes that many people in other nations see as oppressive. Most *Westerners* don't realize that many Muslims think these codes protect and honor women; many followers of Islam don't think their laws oppress women. The most *controversial* of the "protective" laws concerning women include those regulating a woman's "seclusion" (segregation from men), her clothing, and her sexual purity.

ISLAM AND A WOMAN'S HONOR

In March 1997, twenty-two-year-old Muhammad Abed deliberately shot and killed his nineteen-year-old sister Hanan. He received just six months in jail. Why? According to the U.S. State Department's Report on Human Rights Practices for Jordan (1998), "Abed pleaded not guilty to shooting . . . Hanan on the grounds that he had committed the crime in a 'fit of fury' to 'cleanse the family honor' after he heard that she had been 'going out to eat with another man, and was receiving gifts and money from him.' " Hanan's crime was to meet a boyfriend alone in a restaurant and take gifts from him. Abed's crime in

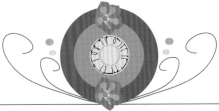

REASONS WOMEN DIE IN HONOR KILLINGS

- She is accused of, suspected of, or seen flirting.

- She speaks to or touches a man who is not a relative.

- She is accused or suspected of premarital sex.

- She is accused or suspected of extramarital affairs.

- She refuses an arranged marriage.

- She asks for a divorce.

- She runs away from an abusive husband.

- She runs away from home.

- She gets pregnant out of wedlock.

- She is raped or otherwise sexually assaulted.

- She marries without parental consent (elopes).

- She befriends a man of a different faith.

- She converts to a different faith.

some countries is not a crime at all. Many Muslims, including some Arab Muslims view "honor killing" as a legitimate way to restore family honor after a daughter or wife has been suspected (note: only suspected, not proven) of dishonorable behavior.

The United Nations Commission on Human Rights documents honor killings like that of Hanan's in several nations, three of which are Arab states: Morocco, Jordan, and Egypt. In other nations, honor killings go unreported, are not documented, or are labeled "suicide." Though nothing in the Qur'an promotes honor killings, many Islamic states and Arab nations who follow Islamic law justify these killings as necessary to preserve a family's respect and dignity when honor laws are breeched.

In Arab lands, a woman's honor is everything. It determines her reputation, her ability to marry, her family's reputation and honor, her family's ability to do business, and her family's social status, among other things. The guidelines for determining honor come from a woman's culture, her family's customs, and the Qur'an. The primary source of a woman's honor is how her community regards her sexual purity (how it *appears*, not necessarily how it is in fact). Muslim's view virgins (women without sexual experience) and faithful wives as honorable; therefore, a woman's sexual purity is guarded at all cost. One way Arab cultures guard female purity is to mandate modest dress codes.

DRESS CODES AND SECLUSION

The Qur'an requires women to cover their hair and behave in a self-controlled, modest manner. The Qur'an, however, identifies only the hair as needing to be covered. Covering the face, body, and hands developed later as cultural customs derived from the need for modesty. Requiring a woman to completely cover her body in public was not originally part of Islam, but this practice is observed in many Arab nations.

CLOTHING THAT COVERS

hijab: A head covering (usually a scarf or veil).

chador: A full-covering shroud worn mostly by rural women.

burqa (or batula): A mask that covers a woman's face.

caftan: A full-length, loose-fitting robe with long sleeves.

abaya: An outer garment made of tightly woven cotton gauze, usually black, that covers the entire body and head. It is worn over other clothing.

jilbab: A cloak or loose outer garment that covers everything but the eyes.

In these nations, when teen girls or women go out in public, their culture (and in some cases, their law) requires them to wear clothing that covers their bodies, arms, legs, ankles, and hair. Arabs consider it inappropriate for a female to reveal the shape of her body to anyone other than her immediate family members or husband (if she is married). They believe that men naturally respond to a woman's hair, body, skin, and smell, and if a woman reveals these to a man, she causes him to act out sexually toward her. In Arab culture, the woman takes responsibility to guard her reputation by not arousing the interest of men. She protects herself by covering her body.

Body coverings for Arab women hide their beauty from men in varying degrees (depending on the laws and culture). This attire can be as simple as a loose scarf worn over the hair while otherwise wearing modest clothing (ankle-length dresses and long sleeves) or a combination of scarves and veils covering the head and face. In some places, Arab women must wear an *abaya*: a loose outer hooded robe, usually black, that drapes the entire body and is worn in public places over their regular clothing.

Hiding her body in loose-fitting clothes or robes isn't the only way an Arab woman protects her honor. She also separates herself from men. In some Arab

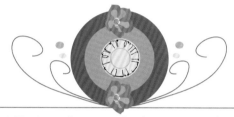

EXCEPTIONS TO THE CLOTHING RULES

Arab women are allowed to wear form-fitting clothing when they are:

- with only their husbands.
- in their homes, around certain immediate family members.
- with other believing women (women who follow the same rules).
- caring for infants or small children who are unaware of sexual issues.

nations, a woman is not allowed to touch, do direct business with, or even make eye contact with a man outside her immediate family.

The most extreme separation happens through a practice called seclusion. *The Oxford Encyclopedia of the Modern Islamic World,* describes seclusion as the practice of confining women to the exclusive company of other women. Arab culture prohibits women and girls (once they reach the onset of *puberty*) from interacting with boys of their age or with men. They go to separate schools, sleep in female-only living quarters at home, and worship in separate places of prayer. Teenage girls don't "hang out" with teenage boys socially, even with chaperones. They are not allowed to participate in sports and any other type of recreation with boys. From pre-adolescence onward, most Arab girls interact

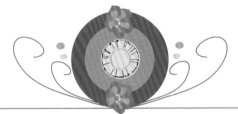

A POSITIVE VIEW OF THE VEIL

In his recently released book **Unholy Wars,** author John Esposito, a professor of Islamic studies at Georgetown University asserts that women who wear the **hijab** "are not passive victims of male-imposed mores but active agents for change. . . . They regard veiling as an authentic practice that preserves their dignity and freedom, enabling them to act and to be treated as persons rather than sex objects."

only with other females. Even when they are grown, many traditional Arab women don't work outside the home, making this separation from males (except those in their immediate family) nearly complete.

Seclusion presents a problem to the modern Arab world. In modern societies that encourage women to pursue education and obtain careers, complete seclusion is impractical. How can women take part in business if they can't interact with men?

The most modern Arab states, while allowing women to work outside the home, handle this issue by maintaining guarded interactions between men and women. Some require a businesswoman to appoint a man to represent her in public business meetings. Others suggest (off the record) that a woman pay a man to use his name (on paper only) to conduct business while completing the actually work behind closed doors herself.

Many businesses allow face-to-face contact between men and women only when it's absolutely necessary. Regardless of strategy, all women in the Arab business world must wear modest, conservative clothing. By far, men run most Arab businesses, so business interactions between men and women are still quite rare.

Some nations (Arab and non-Arab), especially those most influenced by Islamic law, carry these male-female protective measures to an oppressive extreme. These governments (mostly non-Arab but strongly Islamic) forbid women to walk with men in public unless the men are their spouses or immediate family members. Additional laws don't allow a woman to leave her home unless her husband, father, or other male relative goes with her. Still others make it illegal for her to wear nail polish or make-up. In many Arab states, a woman is breaking the law if she consumes alcohol of any kind with a non-related male. If a woman or teen girl disobeys these laws, she can be beaten, tortured, jailed, and in some cases, even killed. At the very least, a woman in the company of a non-related male can be charged with prostitution. A special po-

This modern Arab girl's opportunities may depend on where she lives.

lice force, known as the Mutawwa, or religious police, enforces these laws in Arab states. Though enforced to varying degrees among Arab nations, these laws still exist.

While Arab nations in general aren't this extreme, most have at least some laws that many non-Arabs view as oppressive to women. It is illegal in Saudi Arabia, for example, for a woman to drive a car or ride a bicycle on public roads. Saudi women cannot travel outside Saudi Arabia without a husband's or father's (if she is unmarried) written permission. Many fast-food restaurants in Arab nations will not serve a woman who is not accompanied by a male family member or spouse. Though these laws seem restrictive, many Arabs assert that these regulations protect a woman's purity and honor.

PROTECTING A WOMAN'S SEXUAL PURITY

Because an Arab woman's honor is tied directly to her reputation, Arab laws and customs structure a woman's contact with the opposite gender in ways designed to protect her sexual purity. We've seen how modest dress codes and seclusion protect her. In the next chapter, we'll see how arranged marriages and her role in the family further protect and maintain her reputation for sexual purity.

5

FAMILY LIFE

The family is, by far, the most important social group in Arab nations. But just as public dress codes and social roles vary from nation to nation, so do family values. Simply put, every Arab family is *not* the same. Most Arab families, however, share these things in common:

- a rich cultural and religious heritage
- multi-generational residential living (several generations living together)
- a strong senses of privacy
- a strong sense of loyalty
- close family bonds, even with extended family
- strong senses of duty, honor, and obedience
- respect for elders
- clearly defined roles for men and women

Many Arab families live together with three or four generations under the same roof: the original husband and wife; their unmarried, dependent children;

their married sons, their sons' wives and children; and sometimes a widowed (or divorced) daughter, sister, or mother. Sons tend to stay with their parents, adding their wives and children to the family group. Daughters, when they marry, move away from their families into the husbands' family groups. Can you imagine living with not only your parents and siblings, but your grandparents, your aunts and uncles, and all your cousins, as well? In Arab culture, most families live this way.

Some Arab families live together with extended family members in adjacent houses. Others live together in the same house. The immediate and extended families interact and mingle regularly, involving themselves in each other's lives. Families make all kinds of decisions together, including decisions about work, marriages, education, medical issues, travel, and much more. Rarely do Arab couples or singles make decisions independently from their greater families' influence.

Unlike the rugged individualism we see in North America (every person for his- or herself, individual rights, families living on their own away from relatives, and so on) Arab society emphasizes the importance of the group. Arab culture teaches that the needs of the *group* are more important than the needs of one person.

Let's say, for example, that thirteen-year-old Saja's father wants to build a good relationship with a neighboring family to keep his business growing and to improve his family's social status. To foster good feelings between the two families, Saja's father hints that Saja would make a good bride for the neighboring family's forty-year-old son. Saja wants to go to college and doesn't want to get married, especially to someone so much older, but she won't refuse the marriage proposal. She'll obey her father's wishes because he, like most Arabs, taught his daughter to put her family's needs before her own. The good of the group, in this case Saja's family's reputation and her father's business, means more than the individual need, Saja's desire to remain unmarried.

THE VALUE OF A NAME

Unlike women in many non-Arab countries, an Arab woman does not take her husband's name. Instead, she keeps her family name. Why? Because her family name reveals her origin, heritage, and social status.

Let's say we know an Arab woman whose first name is Sabah. The Arabic word for "mother [of]" is **Umm**, and the Arabic word for "daughter [of]" is **Bint**. If Sabah's full name was **Sabah Imm Muhammad Bint Abu Al-Saud**, her name would mean this in English:

Sabah, mother of Muhammad, daughter of Abu As-Saud.

This woman's first name is Sabah, her son's first name is Muhammad, her father's first name is Abu and her family of origin's last name is Al-Saud. Just by hearing her name, a complete stranger can know three generations of her family tree!

Saja's agreement to marry a man she wouldn't choose reflects not only the Arab principle of group-good-over-individual-good, but it reflects standard Arab family customs.

Because most Arabs practice the Muslim faith, Islamic laws guide most family relationships in Arab lands.

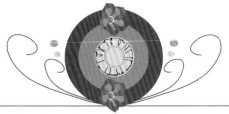

FOUR ASPECTS OF AN ARAB WOMAN'S OBEDIENCE TO HER HUSBAND

1. A wife cannot receive visits or accept gifts from other males without her husband's consent.

2. A woman must yield to her husband's right to control her whereabouts. He can order her to stay home, to not leave the house, to not travel, etc., and she must comply.

3. Arab culture expects a woman to accept her husband's discipline without complaint (including physical punishment, withholding sexual relations, isolation from friends and family, etc.).

4. Unless she has said so in a pre-marital contract, a woman cannot object to her husband taking other wives.

An Arab family shops for food.

Most Arab men eat seperately from the women.

LAWS REGARDING MARRIAGE

- Muslim men can legally marry non-Muslim women; Muslim women cannot marry non-Muslim men.
- Most Arab men are allowed up to four wives; women are allowed only one husband.
- In most Arab societies, a woman's father negotiates a marriage on her behalf (sometimes with and sometimes without her input).
- In some Arab societies a woman can refuse a marriage proposal; in others, she may be forced to marry someone her father chooses despite her objections.
- Arab women cannot legally marry someone in her immediate family (her father, sons, brothers, foster brothers, nephews, or male in-laws); the same rule applies to men.
- A woman, once married, may only associate with other women or men she cannot marry by law (men of her family).
- A married Muslim woman is expected to obey her husband's wishes.
- A Muslim man does not need his wife's consent to take another wife.
- A Muslim marriage is a legal agreement; not a religious sacrament.
- A married Muslim woman retains her name.
- A father may forbid the marriage of his virgin daughter to a man he dislikes or finds unacceptable (for financial, social, or other reasons).
- A man may not marry a woman who is already married.
- A husband is allowed to discipline his wife (even using beatings and marital rape).
- A married woman is not allowed to refuse sex to her husband.

LAWS REGARDING FAMILY FINANCES

- After marriage, an Arab woman's property and dowry belong to her alone (not her husband). She keeps this property even after his death or a divorce.

- Arab women have the right to inherit from deceased relatives, although their inheritances may legally amount to half of what men inherit.

- A Muslim man is legally obligated to provide for his wife's financial and physical needs. The law also requires him to provide for his sons and daughters. This law applies to not only his first wife and children, but equally to all wives and children.

DIVORCE LAWS AND CUSTOMS

- A man in Arab nations, particularly those governed by Islamic law, can divorce his wife by making the statement, "I divorce you," three times. The husband states the phrase twice at one time, then waits three months (or the equivalent of his wife's three menstrual cycles) before stating the phrase the third time (to make sure his wife is not pregnant). If the waiting period proves his wife is not pregnant, he has only to say the statement a third time (after the waiting period) to finalize the divorce. No lawyers or courts get involved.

- Women in most Arab countries are allowed to seek divorce, but only in the cases where she can prove her husband has abused, mistreated, or abandoned her. She must prove her case (with witnesses) to a special court. If her husband contests her request, the court will not grant her a divorce. Even in the cases where a husband beats his wife, the husband can argue that he is following the laws permitting him to

Arab women are often responsible for managing expenses for food and other household necessities.

discipline her. Few courts grant women divorces in these cases. When they do, the courts often force these women to forfeit custody of their children.

• Divorced men and women are allowed to remarry.

Because Arabs place such a high value on family life, privacy, and a woman's honor, most Arab cultures establish strict guidelines for interactions between nonfamily members, too. We discussed some of these in the last chapter, but one surprising custom remains: *it is strictly taboo to enter another person's home without permission.* No matter how urgent the situation, no one (including visiting friends, distant relatives, strangers, and employees who work in the home) is allowed to enter or look into a nonfamily member's house without first obtaining the homeowner's consent. The law exempts children from this rule only until they reach puberty.

Non-Arabs, especially Americans who casually bop into each other's houses, may think this rule extreme or unfair. But Arabs established this rule (based again on the Qur'an) to protect their privacy and the honor of their women. Women needed to be warned that visitors might be entering the house so that they could cover themselves and avoid unacceptable contact with men.

In Arab lands, a man's home is truly his castle, and the laws protect it as such.

DAILY LIFE, EDUCATION, AND RESPONSIBILITIES

You can probably guess by now that most Arab women focus on home responsibilities above all things apart from their faith. A few women establish professional careers and work outside the home, but Arab culture views raising children as a higher calling than career, and especially reveres mothers of multiple sons. Cooking, cleaning, mending, washing—standard domestic chores—remain the woman's domain, though when she is financially able, she can hire servants to do much home care. Arab women also practice needlework, beadwork, basketry, and other crafts. In rural communities, women gather wood, till vegetable plots, tend flocks, cook, fetch water, and care for children.

Education, particularly secondary (high school) education, is something Arab women and Arab culture embraced only in the last hundred years.

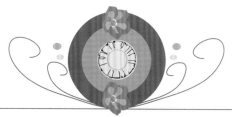

ILLITERACY RATES IN ARAB NATIONS

(a sampling, taken from the 2003 **CIA World Factbook**)

The following percentages represent the number of women in each country over age fifteen who **cannot** read or write:

Bahrain: 15%

Egypt: 43.1%

Iraq: 75.6%

Jordan: 13.7%

Kuwait: 19.3%

Lebanon: 17.8%

Oman: 32.8%

Quatar: 15%

Saudi Arabia: 29.2%

Sudan: 49.5%

Syria: 36%

United Arab Emirates: 19.3%

Yemen: 70%

For comparison, the illiteracy rate in the United States is three percent and for Canada it is three percent (for the total population; female figures were not available).

A Bedouin mother and child.

According to one United Nations study, less than 25 percent of Arab women receive higher education. In some Arab nations, even higher percentages of women cannot even read or write.

Surprisingly to non-Arabs, many Arab women find existing cultural guidelines perfectly acceptable. They view the teachings of their faith and culture as protecting them, not limiting them. They attribute the few practices they see as oppressive to man-made distortions of Islam's teachings, not the faith itself.

Even within Arab society, women disagree over their status. Some Arab women feel valued, loved, and cherished by men in a system that protects them; others feel oppressed and abused. It again depends on the woman's individual experience, her family situation, her cultural heritage, and the laws of the Arab land in which she lives. As we stated in the first chapter, there is no such thing as a "typical Arab woman."

Despite this disagreement, some women in Arab countries have chosen to take stands on several controversial issues and have worked to improve the lives of Arab women in their lands. You'll find their stories in the next chapter.

6

CHANGING THEIR WORLD: ARAB WOMEN WHO ARE MAKING A DIFFERENCE

She's a doctor, *sociologist*, outspoken activist, and author whose novels and books promoting women's rights in Arab and Egyptian societies have been translated into over thirty languages. She's served as an advisor to the United Nations and founded the first legal, independent feminist organization in Egypt. Her opponents, including Anwar Sadat (Egypt's president from 1970 to 1981), charged her with crimes against the state, and she served time in prison. One month after Sadat's assassination she was released and continued her work. Now in her seventies, this advocate for Arab women finds her name on a hit list published by *extremist* organizations in the Middle East. *Fanatics* have targeted her for assassination because she works to improve the situation of women in the Arab world. Who is this pioneer of women's rights in the Middle East? Nawal El Saadawi.

In her own words, provided during a 2002 interview with *Women's Learning Partnership* magazine, another women's rights activist describes what prompted

WHAT ARE HONOR KILLINGS?

Honor killing: When a man kills a female relative (wife, daughter, sister, mother, cousin, etc.) in retaliation for behavior he (or the family) views as dishonorable. Killing the woman accused of dishonorable behavior (anything that compromises her reputation) is believed to restore the family's honor.

her to start working toward eliminating violence against women. The following incident occurred when she was just a young lawyer:

> About twenty years ago, a woman came to my office requesting help. She told me that her husband had murdered their fifteen-year-old daughter who was pregnant as a result of rape. Her husband was sentenced to only six months in jail, claiming that he killed the girl to vindicate the family's honor. However, this woman revealed that her husband was in fact the rapist. The court believed her husband [his denial] and did not investigate the crime any further. I decided then and there that I would do my best to change laws that ignore or cover up crimes against women. And that is how I became one of the leaders in the campaign to eradicate honor crimes.

Nawal El Saadawi

Nawal El Mountawakel is an Olympic gold medalist from Morocco.

Today, Jordan-born lawyer, author, and human rights activist Asma Khader, the young lawyer who felt helpless to assist the woman in the episode described above, serves as the Minister of State and Government Spokesperson for the Jordanian Cabinet. The United Nations Development Program awarded Khader the 2003 Poverty Eradication Award for her work toward ending poverty for women and children with Jordan's National Network for Poverty Alleviation. The founder and president of Mizan (a legal group that advocates human rights), this dedicated activist uses her considerable talent and skill to promote justice for women, especially in legal issues concerning rights abuses. She is a leading advocate in Jordan working to make laws that would make it illegal for men to conduct honor killings.

As she summarizes in a recent press release, the goal of her work for women is to fulfill her dream to "see all people around me living in peace, dignity, freedom and enjoying their lives."

In some ways it resembled a scene out of any political campaign: a candidate discussing issues with voters, greeting them with smiles, handshakes, kisses, and occasional small talk. In other ways, the scene seemed surreal: a goat-hair tent home; people in flowing black robes; women with customary tattoos on their faces; tribal elders offering their support. The truly remarkable thing about this image is that the candidate is a Bedouin woman—the first Bedouin woman ever to run for Jordan's representative Parliament. Bedouin custom traditionally separates women from men, and most Bedouin women would never shake the hand of an unknown male. (Islam forbids Muslim men to touch another man's wife, even her hand.) The thought of a Bedouin woman running for public office, and shaking men's hands, would have been unheard of even a decade ago.

Though laws in Jordan allow women to drive, travel, and pursue education, Bedouin culture is more traditional, a fact illustrated by the low numbers of women involved in public life and politics. Only one in seven Jordanian women holds a job. By the time of the 2003 election discussed above, the Jordanian government had granted only four high-level positions of influence to women: one Cabinet member spot; one judgeship, one Parliament member spot, and one air force pilot position. Yet Fayza Nueimi greets her supporters with the charm of a seasoned politician.

"It won't be a problem if I lose the election," the Associated Press quotes Nueimi as saying in an article dated June 16, 2003, "because I'd have achieved my other goal, which is breaking the taboo on Bedouin women contesting the poll, and I'm sure many women in my area would run in the next polls in 2007."

One more "activist," whom we'll call Raw'ah (not her real name), lives today with her husband in Western Sudan where he serves as a high level diplomat. Both she and her spouse obtained advanced educational degrees and lived in the United States for several years. As a practical nurse and a woman born and raised in Sudan, Raw'ah understands the pain and potential consequences of female circumcision (sometimes called female genital mutilation), a practice routinely carried out in Asia, Indonesia, the Middle East, and many African nations.

Female circumcision is a surgical procedure done to a girl anywhere from a month after her birth to when she becomes pregnant with her first child (depending on custom), during which a *midwife* or medical practitioner removes either a part, some, or all of her external genital organs (the labia and clitoris). Most frequently completed when a girl is between six and twelve years old, the procedure can be done with or without her consent, with or without local anesthesia or pain medication, with or without clean instruments, and with or without proper follow-up care—again depending on local custom. Many girls die or have life-long complications because of the procedure itself, excessive bleeding, infection, or botched procedures.

COMPLICATIONS OF FEMALE CIRCUMCISION

Amnesty International, an international human rights organization, cites these physical complications of FGM (female genital mutilation):

- post-surgical infection

- death from shock, organ damage, infection, or hemorrhage

- life long intermittent bleeding

- chronic infections

- abscesses

- small tumors

- excessive scarring

- pelvic inflammation

- urinary tract problems

- infertility

- infections in the uterus and vagina

- spreading of HIV (from unclean instruments)

- pain and tearing during intercourse

Assia Djebar is an award-winning poet, novelist, and film director from Algeria.

After the midwife (often unskilled and with little training) cuts away the girl's private parts, she stitches the remaining tissue closed so that the girl no longer has a vaginal opening. The stitching leaves only a tiny hole, usually about the diameter of matchstick, through which the girl can urinate and release her menstrual bleeding when she comes of age. She usually remains this way until her wedding night, when she is forced open (gently or brutally, depending on her husband).

Most cultures that still practice female circumcision claim to do so to protect a girl's honor (and her family's honor) and to make her more pleasing to a prospective husband.

Though the Islam religion and Arab nations do not require female circumcision, the practice continues by tribal and family custom. According to Amnesty International, high percentages of women living in Djibouti (90 to 98 percent), Egypt (97 percent), Somalia (98 percent), and northern Sudan (89 percent)—four Arab nations—experienced this painful procedure, most in childhood. Our activist, Raw'ah, recounts her circumcision, which she went through when she was five years old, in Hanny Lightfoot-Klein's book entitled *Prisoners of Ritual: An Odyssey into Female Circumcision in Africa*:

> I came from a bad, bad village in [western Sudan], where they scrape off everything. There is not even skin left to sew up and they tie your legs together for forty days, until a scar forms. There is nothing left with which to feel. . . .
>
> I will not do this to my daughter. I have told my family that even if I have ten daughters, I will not do it to one of them. I see no sense in it. . . . Everyone tries to persuade me that it must be done to my daughter, saying that no one will marry her, but I tell them I don't care. Let her get old enough to decide what she wants for herself. . . .

Raw'ah, though not officially a political "activist," is an advocate for her daughters. She daily undergoes a quiet, personal campaign to resist the bar-

Nazli Gad El Mawla: doctor, pioneer of oncology medical field (Egypt)

Assia Djebar: award-winning novelist, poet, and film director (Algeria)

Ghadah Al-Samman: journalist (Syria)

Fadia Faqir: author, award-winning editor, lecturer (Jordan)

Nawal El Moutawakel: athlete, Olympic Gold Medalist (Morocco)

Maha Garagash: award-winning filmmaker (United Arab Emirates)

Rasha Al-Sabah: politician and educator (Kuwait)

Nabiha Gueddana: politician and professor of medicine (Tunisia)

Rania Al-Baz: TV show host, advocate against domestic violence (Saudi Arabia)

Fadia Faqir is an author and award-winning editor from Jordan.

Many modern Arab women have made great achievements.

baric, unnecessary cultural practice that more than nine out of ten women in her country undergo. Her battle to change the lives of her daughters is every bit as courageous as the public campaigns waged by her better-known counterparts involved in legal and political advocacy in other lands.

These four women—Egyptian activist Nawal El Saadawi, Jordanian lawyer Asma Khader, Bedouin politician Fayza Nueimi, and Sudanese mother Raw'ah—seek to change the world for women in their corners the globe. Their lives and actions represent only a few of the many outstanding, remarkable women who dare to stand up to unfair traditions, injustice, or discriminatory laws. By doing what she can, with the talents, resources, education, and training she's been given, each paves the way toward a brighter future for their daughters and other Arab women.

Despite the brave works of such courageous women, much still needs to be done. As we'll see in the next chapter, women in Arab lands face hurdles and issues non-Arabs can only imagine.

7

UNFINISHED BUSINESS: ISSUES AND CONTROVERSIES FACING ARAB WOMEN TODAY

A husband murdered his wife after dreaming that she was unfaithful.

A woman tried to leave her husband after enduring ten years of violent domestic abuse. A friend of her mother's killed the abused woman as she met with her lawyer.

After older brothers repeatedly raped her causing her to become pregnant, Rofayda Qaoud quietly gave up her child for adoption. Then her mother handed her a razor and encouraged her to commit suicide. The Palestinian teenager refused. So on the night of January 27, 2003, thinking to protect her other children by restoring family honor, the mother entered her sleeping daughter's room, forced a plastic bag over her head, and slit the teen's wrists. When, after several cries of "No, Mother, no!" Rofayda's body went limp, the older woman bludgeoned her daughter's head with a stick. In Rofayda's mother's mind, the twenty horrible minutes it took to kill her daughter was worth the honor her death restored to the family name.

In 1998, a twenty-eight-year-old Egyptian woman secretly fell in love with and married a man from a lower (poorer) social class. When her family found out, her brothers beat her and her father charged her with "illegal marriage" (marriage without family consent). Fearing the family might try to punish her, the police sent the young woman to prison for "protective custody." Five years later, she is still in prison. Why? The police will not release her until she can find someone to guarantee she won't be harmed. Her family won't make that guarantee, and the Egyptian police won't release her to anyone but a family member. At the writing of this book, she is still in prison.

CROSS-CULTURAL CHILD ABDUCTIONS

One area of women's rights often overlooked in Arab lands is the right of parentage. Foreign women sometimes marry Arab men. After relocating to his homeland (an Arab country), some women discover that their children belong to their husbands more than they do to them. If a woman attempts to leave her husband's country, most Arab laws prohibit her from taking the children with her; custody goes to the father. Of all countries involved in cross-culture child custody cases with the United States in 2003, five of the top ten were countries in the Middle East, including Jordan, Egypt, and Saudi Arabia.

In 2003, a sixteen-year-old Jordanian girl left home for three days to be with a man she loved and wanted to marry. After her family discovered her absence, they planned to have her arrested upon her return. When police arrested her and medical tests confirmed she was still a virgin, officials agreed to release the girl to her family if the family promised they would not injure or hurt her in any way. Her father assured authorities his daughter would be safe. Minutes after arriving home from the police station, the girl's eighteen-year-old brother shot and killed her.

These accounts, documented by *National Geographic*, the *Philadelphia Inquirer* (November 21, 2003), Human Rights Watch, and the U.S. State Department (respectively), illustrate just a few of the ongoing challenges women face in Arab lands. Startling statistics provided by Amnesty International (AI) summarize the plight of women worldwide: as of 2003, fifty-four countries still have laws that actively discriminate against women; seventy-nine countries do not outlaw domestic violence; and 127 countries have no laws against *sexual harassment*. AI estimates that one in every three women worldwide suffers rape, attack, or assault sometime in her lifetime. The United Nations reports that more than half of all Arab women remain illiterate and that they have the lowest level of political participation in the region.

Statistics alone don't tell the tale. Consider these current laws:

- In Jordan, Saudi Arabia, and Egypt, wife-beating and marital rape are legal.
- In Syria, a husband can confine his wife to the country and restrict her travel.
- In Egypt, Iraq, Libya, Jordan, Morocco, Oman, and Yemen, husbands must provide written permission for their wives to travel abroad.

- In Saudi Arabia, a woman's closest male relative (spouse or father) must provide written permission for her to travel to other parts of Saudi Arabia beyond her hometown.

Arab women trail men in other areas, too:

- Women made up only twenty-nine percent of the Arab world's work force in 2000.
- Nearly twice as many Arab women are unemployed as are men.
- Arab women's participation in government is still very low.

While these stories, laws, and statistics make the Arab woman's plight look grim, Arab women are making some progress in their cultures.

In Saudi Arabia, for example, for the first time in history the Saudi government is planning to issue identification cards to women (the government listed women on their husbands' or fathers' cards in the past). In 2001, Bahrain's rulers established a Supreme Council for Women to promote women's rights and to encourage their participation in public life. In 2002, the United Arab Emirates (UAE) filled its technology colleges with more than 70 percent women. Statistics cite that 99 percent of all UAE girls go to school at some point in their lives. In Kuwait, the government at least attempted to pass a bill allowing women to vote and run for public office in 2003 (the bill failed by two votes).

The United Nations provides additional encouraging news:

- The life expectancy of women in the Arab world has increased three years since 1990.
- Maternal mortality (women who die in childbirth) rates have gone down.

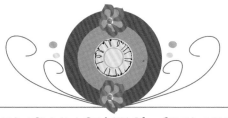

ARAB WOMEN IN POLITICS—ROOM TO GROW

According to the United Nations Economic and Social
Commission for Western Asia, in 2003:

• women held less than five percent of the seats in Arab
parliamentary governments;

• few Arab countries had yet given women the right to vote or
run for public office;

• women held less than three percent of ministerial (government) posts, and those that did were usually lower-level
management.

• The literacy rate of women in the region increased ten percent in the last
ten years.

• In 2000, nine Arab girls for every ten Arab boys went to primary and secondary schools.

So, the news for Arab women is both good and bad. Yes, women in Arab
lands are making great strides for establishing equal rights and fair treatment

This sign posted in an Arabic country warns visitors to dress and act appropriately.

under the laws of their various nations. But much work still needs to be done. Organizations like the United Nations, Amnesty International, and Human Rights Watch help promote healthier views of women and work to protect women worldwide. The greatest change, however, happens one life at a time. That kind of change begins with education.

Think for a moment about all you've read in this book. What have you learned? How has your thinking changed because of what you've learned? With whom will you talk about these issues? What can you do to help others better understand people who differ from them?

Maybe you can write a report for school or send a letter to your local newspaper. Or maybe you can just talk with a friend. If each of us took a stand against the injustices we see or learn about in this world, the world could become a better place for us all. Learning about women in Arab lands is a good place to begin.

FURTHER READING

Baker, William G. *The Cultural Heritage of Arabs, Islam, and the Middle East.* Dallas, Tex.: Brown Books Publishing Group, 2003.

Ellis, Deborah. *Breadwinner.* Toronto, Ont.: Groundwood Books, 2001.

Ellis, Deborah. *Parvana's Journey.* Toronto, Ont.: Groundwood Books, 2003.

Farndorn, John. *1000 Things You Should Know About Geography.* Broomall, Penn.: Mason Crest Publishers, 2003.

Hodges, Rick. *What Muslims Think, How They Live.* Broomall, Penn.: Mason Crest Publishers, 2004.

Khouri, Norma. *Honor Lost: Love and Death in Modern-Day Jordan.* New York: Washington Square Press, 2004.

Latifa. *My Forbidden Face: Growing Up Under the Taliban: A Young Woman's Story.* New York: Hyperion, 2001.

McCoy, Lisa. *Bahrain.* Broomall, Penn.: Mason Crest Publishers, 2003.

Nye, Naomi Shihab. *Habibi.* New York: Simon and Shuster, 1999.

Nye, Naomi Shihab. *19 Varieties of Gazelle: Poems of the Middle East.* New York: Greenwillow, 2002.

Queen Noor. *Leap of Faith: Memoirs of an Unexpected Life.* New York: Miramax, 2003.

Sasson, Jean. *Princess: A True Story of Life Behind the Veil in Saudi Arabia.* Woodstock, N.J.: Windsor-Brooke Books, 2001.

Staples, Suzanne Fisher. *Haveli.* New York: Random House, 1993.

Whitehead, Kim. *Islam: The Basics.* Broomall, Penn.: Mason Crest Publishers, 2004.

FOR MORE INFORMATION

Amnesty International: Working to Protect Human Rights Worldwide
www.amnesty.org

Arab Female
arabfemale.com

Arab Gateway: Women in the Arab World
www.al-bab.com/arab/women.htm

Arab World Woman
ellearab.com/s/arabworldwoman

OneWorld.net (an information resource devoted to worldwide human rights)
www.oneworld.net

The Islam Project
www.theislamproject.org

UNIFEM: The United Nations Development Fund for Women
www.unifem.org

Women's Court: The Permanent Arab Court to Resist Violence Against Women
www.arabwomencourt.org

Women's Human Rights Net
www.whrnet.org

Women's Human Rights Resources
www.law-lib.utoronto.ca/diana

Women Living Under Muslim Laws
wluml.org/english

World News Kids
wnkids.com

Publisher's note:
The Web sites listed on these pages were active at the time of publication. The publisher is not responsible for Web sites that have changed their addresses or discontinued operation since the date of publication. The publisher will review and update the Web sites upon each reprint.

GLOSSARY

abaya A loose black robe from head to toe; traditionally worn by Muslim women.

abstain To refrain deliberately and often with an effort of self-denial from an action or practice.

adhan The Muslim call to prayer.

advocated To plead the cause of another.

authoritative Showing evident authority.

civic Of or relating to a citizen, a city, citizenship, or civil affairs.

civil rights The nonpolitical rights of a citizen.

colonial Having to do with a territory that has kept ties to a parent nation.

controversial Generating argument or debate; characteristic of a position that some people will be inclined not to accept.

convert A person who has been converted to another religious or political belief.

doctrine A principle of law established through past decisions.

dowry The money, goods, or estate that a woman brings to her husband in marriage.

extremist A person who holds extreme views.

fanatics People marked by excessive enthusiasm for and intense devotion to a cause or idea.

feminist A person who advocates equal rights for women.

gynecologist A doctor who deals with diseases and routine physical care of the reproductive system of women.

Islam The religious faith of Muslims including belief in Allah as the sole deity and in Muhammad as his prophet.

martyrs People who decide to suffer and/or die for the sake of faith or principles.

midwife Person whose work is helping women in childbirth.

mosque A building used for public worship by Muslims.

muezzin A Muslim crier who calls the hour of daily prayers.

nomad A member of a people who have no fixed residence but move from place to place usually seasonally and within a well-defined territory.

patriarch The male leader of a clan or family.

promiscuity The act of indulging in casual and indiscriminate sexual relations.

puberty The period of physical development when sexual reproduction first becomes possible.

sexual harassment Any form of sexual attention that is unwelcome.

sociologist A person who studies the institutions and development of human society

stereotype A fixed and often negative impression of all members of an ethnic, religious or other group

surreal Resembling a dream

tenets Principles, beliefs, or doctrines.

Westerners Natives or inhabitants of Europe or the United States who advocate the adoption of western European culture.

INDEX

PICTURE CREDITS

Artville: p. 6
Michelle Bouch: pp. 16, 36, 83, 84, 88, 91
Comstock: p. 46
Corel: pp. Cover, 19, 22, 28, 30 41, 56, 64, 71, 72, 75, 78, 97
Map Resources: cover
Photo Alto: p. 92
Photo Disk: pp. 52, 101
Benjamin Stewart: cover
World Portraits: p. 12

BIOGRAPHIES

Joan Esherick is a full-time author, freelance writer, and professional speaker who lives with her family outside of Philadelphia, Pennsylvania. She is the author of fourteen books, including Our Mighty Fortress: Finding Refuge in God (Moody Press, 2002), The Big Picture: The Bible's Story in Thirty Short Scenes, and multiple books with Mason Crest Publishers. Joan has also contributed dozens of articles to national print periodicals. For more information about her you can visit her web site at www.joanesherick.com.

Dr. Mary Jo Dudley is the director of Cornell University's Gender and Global Change Department, which focuses on the evolving role of gender around the world. She is also the associate director of Latin American Studies at Cornell.